FUTURE BUSINESS

A CRESTWOOD HOUSE BOOK

LIBRARY OF CONGRESS CATALOGING IN PUBLICATION DATA

Abels, Harriette Sheffer.
  Future business.

  (Our Future world)
  Bibliography: p.
  SUMMARY: Discusses the foreseeable evolution of today's businesses as they adapt to future society.
  1. Business enterprises--Juvenile literature. 2. Industry--Juvenile literature. (1. Business enterprises) I. Schroeder, Howard. II. Vista III Design. III. Title. IV. Series.
HF5353.A23   338.7   80-14859
ISBN 0-89686-081-7 (lib. bdg.)
ISBN 0-89686-090-6 (pbk.)

INTERNATIONAL STANDARD BOOK NUMBERS:	**LIBRARY OF CONGRESS CATALOG CARD NUMBER:**
0-89686-081-7 Library Bound 0-89686-090-6 Paperback	80-14859

CRESTWOOD HOUSE

P.O. Box 3427, Hwy. 66 South
Mankato, MN 56001

FUTURE BUSINESS

BY **HARRIETTE S. ABELS**

ILLUSTRATED BY:
VISTA III DESIGN

EDITED BY:
DR. HOWARD SCHROEDER
Professor in Reading and Language Arts
Dept. of Elementary Education
Mankato State University

GRAPHIC DESIGN BY:
MARK E. AHLSTROM

ART DIRECTION BY:
RANDAL M. HEISE

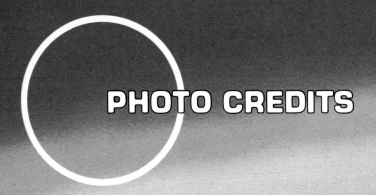

PHOTO CREDITS

In the past, predicting the future was an intellectual game. Sometimes the predictions came true. More often they didn't.

Today there is a new branch of science developing throughout the world. The people working in this field are called "Futurists." They are recognized as top experts in their fields. No one can say positively what the world will be like in the twenty-first century. But the Futurists are making some exciting predictions.

THE INDUSTRIAL REVOLUTION

People first appeared on earth about three million years ago. Things went along slowly at first. A million years to learn how to make tools; another million and a half years to learn about fire; 400,000 more years to understand farming and crops. In the next few thousand years people slowly became more intelligent and civilized.

Then came the nineteenth century and the Industrial Revolution. That did it. The world went through a kind of time warp. Things speeded up in a way they never had before.

Life on earth has changed in every way since the Industrial Revolution — politically, economically, and socially. And according to the futurists, scientists who study the future, the best part is still to come.

The beginning of the Industrial Revolution saw the building of giant steel mills. Railroads were built everywhere, with millions and millions of miles of

It is hard to imagine, that only a brief time ago (in the historical sense) the only "business" was sitting around the fire discussing the hunting prospects.

tracks. The petroleum industry became the back-bone of the economy. Soon we moved into the automobile generation and had the everyday use of electricity.

The second giant step forward came after World War II. Light metals, such as aluminum, came into general use, along with plastics and electronics. The routine use of the airplane, and the entire aero-space industry, developed in a few short years.

The two greatest discoveries were nuclear fis-sion and our latest marvel, the computer.

What do the futurists see ahead? Things that only the scientists understand at this point: in-dustrial microbiology, bionics, biochemical indus-tries, mariculture, enhanced bioconversion, com-posites and nuclear fusion, and the greatest change of all, the way these new inventions and discoveries will affect our life style.

> Our industry has been both a blessing and a curse. It has made us the mightiest nation in the world, with the highest standard of living. It has also polluted air, water and land, causing sickness and death for thousands of people, as well as damaging wildlife.

8

CHANGING VALUES

For the first time since the beginning of the Industrial Revolution, peoples' personal and social values are turning away from getting and keeping material things, and going back to improving the quality of life. People are beginning to think and care about other people. As we move toward the next century, male and female roles are becoming less different. Race and religious problems and

differences are slowly fading. More of this will come about as the changes in work habits and the work force evolve. New technology will require less of our natural resources and less physical energy than we use now.

Until the present time, growth in business has been in areas of products and physical labor. This will change to the area of getting and giving knowledge and information. As our population growth problems ease and our average life span gets longer, there will be less need for new consumer goods. When the standard of living improves, the trend is not always toward "taking more" but toward more choice and selection in the goods and services we already use.

NEW FIELDS

Many of the major industries that the futurists foresee in the twenty-first century have already begun today. For instance, many futurists think that one of the major industries will be "do-goodism."

The last twenty years have seen great steps forward in human relations. We are finally beginning to learn we can love and get along with people of different races or religions other than our own.

That is, people making a career out of helping other people. Today we have social workers, as well as private charities, but neither of these groups is large enough or varied enough to be considered an industry. By the year 2000 it is expected that this will change. "Do-goodism" will become a major field with millions of paid jobs in areas not yet begun.

One of the largest industries will be in knowledge and information. Libraries are already changing from the quiet reading rooms of the past to large storage centers of information. By the next century this industry will require hundreds of thousands of people to read, research, interpret and write all of the covered knowledge. They will condense the flood of new information that will pile up much faster than it does today. Knowledge will be centered in frequent newsletters and tapes for all types of national organizations, local groups, and ordinary individuals.

Today, when we want to see the past, we go to a museum. They have artifacts (old tools or objects), and long written descriptions about what life was like in ancient times. In the future, futurists see a huge industry in the field of simulated or imitation environments — that is, a combination of museums and Disneyland.

These imitation environments will recreate the past down to the smallest detail. Visitors will come to live for a short time in the way that their ancestors lived. These places will be put together by museum specialists, historians, designers, computer experts, and roboteers. They will skillfully recreate the dynasties of China, the glories of ancient Greece, the magnificence of the seventeenth cen-

As social service grows in size, we will have major industries serving giant world problems. One of these is food distribution, for which we may have a worldwide "charity" corporation.

13

Travel is one of the major
industries in the world today, and it is
one of the best ways to get to know other people.

tury French court and the harsh beginnings of the Massachusetts Bay Colony. Instead of just reading about our past it will be possible to actually relive it somewhat as we can do today in Williamsburg, Virginia.

In the generation of computers and automation that lies ahead, people will spend more time at play than at work. It isn't hard to see that this will cause a great boon in the tourist industry.

As it becomes easier for everyone in the world to travel, getting ready to travel will become more involved. Tour directors will have long meetings with their customers, showing them audio-visual programs of the sights they will see. Today, some tour companies send a person along on the tour who is well informed in a particular field, such as wine making or archaeology. In the future, it will be common to have private meetings with an historian, an archaeologist, or an expert in the fields of music or art, so that the tourist may have an in-depth conversation with an expert.

Once you arrive at your destination, it will be possible to take part in the regional crafts of the area. Not only will the tourist walk through a factory or bazaar, where they are weaving rugs or making pottery, but there will be skillful teachers present to help the tourists make something of their own. Today it is possible to travel to France and take a special cooking course. This idea will be expanded until it will be possible to have a home filled with objects that you have made yourself in the place from which they originally came.

Because there will be so much leisure time, dozens of new industries will pop up that we cannot even imagine today. A number of these will probably be in the field of sports. Just as tennis, racquet ball and disco dancing have become popular in the recent past, so other sports, games and leisure activities will become major industries in the future.

Of course, some of the new industries will be involved with actual products. At the moment, one of our greatest concerns is the production of an alternate or artificial fuel supply. Futurists expect that within the next twenty years we shall have the beginning of some type of fuel production from plants. It may be possible to make fuel from forests and agricultural wastes which will give us the beginnings of a new industry. The making of hydrogen on a large scale, by using a photochemical process, might also work.

We'd still use insects and other organisms to make products for us. For instance, bees are still our source of honey, and silkworms are the only known way for us to get real silk cloth. There is some thought of increasing this type of production past anything now known, especially in the developing countries.

Since the Industrial Revolution, the structure of business and industry has remained very much the

This plant, Euphorbia Tirucalli, has a milky sap which can be distilled into gasoline. In the future we may be growing our gasoline in this way.

same. As each new product or invention came along, it was produced or manufactured in very much the same way as everything else. With the change in our goals should also come a change in our methods. As we shift from a society concerned about things, to a society concerned about people, business and industrial methods must shift along with it.

THE NEAR FUTURE

From now until the twenty-first century business and industry will probably be more concerned with refining and expanding present businesses rather than starting new ones. The energy crisis has forced business as well as government to rethink the use of some earth resources.

In the next twenty years we shall probably see a return to extensive coal mining. Because coal mining and oil burning produce enormous amounts of

air and industrial pollution, coal mining had become almost a dead industry. Today, with the ability to clean up wastes, coal once again has become an attractive form of energy. This probably will not last. Using coal will be a stop-gap solution until we can discover and produce other forms of energy. Although solar energy will be more available in the near future, it will not become a major industry for years to come. Economically, a shortage of oil in the near future will be a tremendous aid to the coal mining industry.

This type of slow change will also affect the automobile industry. It will be many years before a practical electric car will be ready for general use. In the meantime, our present automobiles will be changed. The basic fuel source will still be gasoline; but with changes such as adding alcohol to produce gasohol, and with changes in the computerized systems in cars to give us greater gas economy, we will slowly be moving toward the day when we will need less and less oil based fuels.

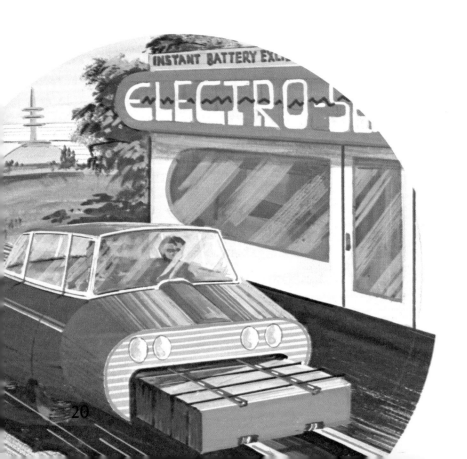

20

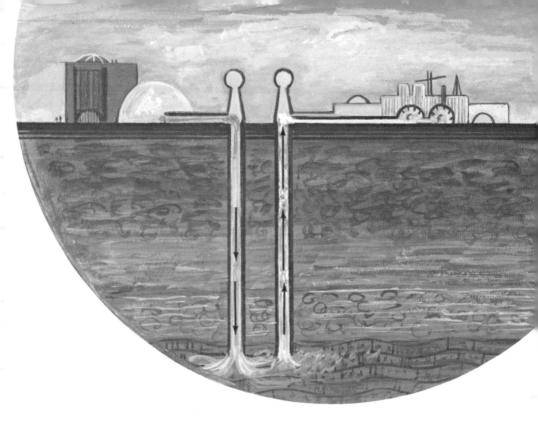

Another form of energy that is slowly moving into the big business field is the one called "hot rocks" or a geothermal form of energy. It combines the know-how we already have about drilling oil wells with geology, chemistry, and hydrology.

A hole is drilled three to six miles deep into the earth. There, drillers find rocks heated by the earth's core to 300 degrees farenheit (150 degrees celsius) or higher. Two holes are drilled near each other. Water is forced into one hole. From the other hole, steam comes out. This steam is called "thermal energy," and it can be used for heating, or to run machines.

A car of the future may have a battery pack, which can be changed just by driving onto a track, pushing the old battery out the back while running a new one in the front.

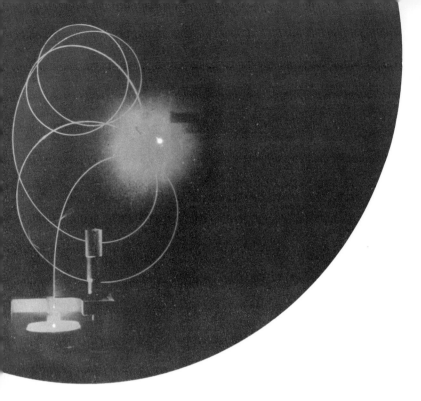

Another field that has become popular in the past few years is the field of fiber optics, sending messages on a beam of light. When fiber optics was first invented it was thought that it would become a major force by the year 1990. Instead, it has grown faster than any other technological industry, and is already hard at work in the communications field. Messages travel at higher speed and in greater volume than was ever possible with electricity using copper wire.

In 1977 the Bell Telephone System first began field tests using fiber optics in their telephone system. Today, only a few short years later, the same principles have changed the computer field.

The discovery of fiber optics may eventually permit television transmission to be tied in with every other form of communication.

Probably the fastest-growing group of industries in the near future will be those connected in some way with automation and computers. But the average worker's attitude toward machines must go through a complete change. Until now, in the years of the Industrial Revolution, the average worker has feared his machine. Workers in industry were not only afraid of the machines for physical reasons (and rightly so in many cases), but workers also feared that the machines would eventually take over most jobs and workers would be left without a way of earning a living.

Up to this point, the man working at the machine has also looked upon that machine as a slave. When someone owns slaves, they always fear that someday the slaves will revolt and turn on them. But if the worker realizes that the machine is his partner, and not a slave, and is there to help him and to make his life easier, then the worker and the machine can work together.

A trucker driving his rig is working with a machine that could be dangerous. But truckers get to know their rigs and develop a relationship with them almost as they would with another person.

Therefore, the rigs become the trucker's partner in business. The same is true of a construction worker driving a caterpiller, or a professional seamstress and a sewing machine.

The trucker's rig will someday be automated. So will the caterpiller and the sewing machine. But if the workers understand that these steps are progress, and will help to make their machines more of a partner in making their life easier, then this future step in the Industrial Revolution will be a success.

THE FAR FUTURE

One of the major industries in the far future will be the mining of space: sending back minerals and metals mined from the asteroids and the moon. But it will be many decades before we are ready to begin these space operations. In the meantime, earth will start running short of these needed elements. Scientists are already preparing to partly solve this problem by mining the sea.

One day mining companies will be sending prospectors to the moon, and even to the asteroids, looking for minerals. We will mine the minerals and bring them back to earth or to space colonies.

Mineral prospectors will also search the ocean bottoms
for new sources of raw materials.

Living on the floor of the sea has already
become a reality. In the oil industry steel "houses"
have been built over oil or gas wells on the sea bottom at depths as great as three thousand feet. Inside
this building the pressure is kept at sea level. When
it is necessary to do repair work, men are lowered
from the surface to the building in a transfer chamber. The pressure in the transfer chamber is kept at

sea level so that the pressure on their bodies never changes. It is expected that by the turn of the twenty-first century oil companies will be using these pressure houses all the time.

Being able to live on the sea floor will also give a great push to the mining industry. Parts of the ocean floor are covered with black, mineral-rich lumps the size of lemons. In some places they are as thick as a carpet. These lumps are mainly manganese, but they also have some iron, nickel, copper, and cobalt in them.

It is also known that there are other mineral deposits that contain calcium phosphate, a valuable mineral that is used in making fertilizer (food for our soil). As the trend in recent years has been away from using chemical fertilizers and returning to natural ones, calcium phosphate is becoming more and more desirable. Our present land sources of calcium phosphate will run out before the year 2000.

It is also known that there is coal under the ocean, as well as lead, zinc, and possibly uranium that we need for nuclear fuel. And just as an added bonus, off the coastlines of California and Alaska there are underwater gold fields. Before we begin to mine in space, we shall surely mine underwater.

As we move into the twenty-first century, progress will move at an even faster rate. Skilled workers will have to return to school as many as four times in their lives to be totally retrained in their own field. The technical knowledge in every industry will become out of date that quickly.

As the workers' life styles change, adult schooling will be more common, and special guidance counseling systems will be offered and paid

In the near future we may see many new kinds of machinery for mining and locating minerals on the ocean bottom. As this business grows it will also bring a need for many new job skills.

for by industry. Teachers in these classes will probably be part-time educators who are professional and industrial leaders. Many of the courses may be taught right at the working place, using mail courses or learning machines. Special libraries in the factory lunchroom and rest areas will be common.

As industry moves in this direction, the whole structure of industrial life will change. The workers themselves, working in teams, will make their own production decisions. Factory work will be reorganized so that the owners and workers will make decisions together. As automation moves ahead, many of the workers will work at home. Most workers will probably hold two jobs or go to school part of the time. The need to keep learning through your whole life will be an accepted idea.

Even the unions and unionism will probably go through a drastic change. The workers will play a basic role in the union's program. Unions will train their new workers in the local community colleges. Bargaining about wages, hours, and other things between the union leaders and the employers will continue; but they will become joint problem-solving task forces. The books, data, and papers of the company will be opened to labor as well as to the heads of the companies.

SPACE INDUSTRY

Finally, business and industry will move into space. The site for an industry in space will probably depend on the special environment needed for that particular industrial process. For instance, solar energy will be easier to come by on the sunward side of the planetoid belts. An industrial operation in the inner solar system would be built near the raw materials needed to feed it, or in the parts of the solar system where it would be easiest to build the space environment needed for it.

We do know that industry in space will be in a gravity-free environment. It will also have to be a matter-free (high vacuum) environment. The radiation will have to be controlled, as well as the wide range of temperatures. Some industries will need the cold of nearly absolute zero, while others will be interested in high temperatures.

Some products are already being thought of for manufacture in space. They are ball bearings, high-purity crystals such as super-size diamonds, medical vaccines, and long, high-strength filament materials.

Space factories will not be the same as our factories on Earth. The early ones will be movable space labs. They will ride into space in the cargo hold of a shuttle ship and later return to the Earth. These small space factories will produce limited products — probably vaccines, crystals, and fragile materials such as thin films and special highly engineered items.

Space factories that can run continuously will probably be the next step. At that point the space shuttle will put a completely manned module in orbit with a few technicians to run it. The space shuttle will then bring up more technicians, replace-

A factory in space may look like this.
Long banks of solar collectors attached to it
provide all the power that is needed.

ments for the life-support system, and new raw materials. When the shifts change in these space factories and the workers return to earth, they will bring their finished products with them.

The third step will be to put another module in orbit alongside the first one. They will be connected

Here we see a production manager checking output in a space factory, while two shuttle pilots check their loading instructions for a return trip.

with ropes and spacesuited technicians will travel between them. The final step will be to join the two space modules directly.

Over the years, this space factory will probably grow just like any factory does on earth when it needs more room. Eventually the time will come when it will cost too much to deliver the raw materials and construction materials into space from earth. At that point, we will begin gathering the raw materials from space.

One day we will have perfected the closed ecological life-support system. That will mean that people can spend their whole lives in space, never having to return to earth unless they want to. By that time we should be making exploratory trips into the planetoid belt and onto the nearest planets. The raw material available for our industries will be never-ending.

FUTURE OFFICE

We all know what a typical businessperson looks like, they wear a well-made suit — with a shirt and tie or a neat blouse. When they leave their house in morning, they go to an office. In the office is a big desk filled with papers and a telephone with a lot of buttons. They have at least one secre-

Today's office may be highly automated, but it still requires a vast amount of personal attention by workers in the office, as seen here.

tary, and if they are very important they have two or three.

Tomorrow's businessperson won't look like that at all. If they have an office it will be small and will probably be in their own home. They may have a great many secretaries, but the chances are they won't see them very often. The secretaries will probably work at home after a short training period in the main office. The company will have remote

Tomorrow's secretary may work at home, using an electronic communicator to "talk" to the office.

dictation unit computer terminals installed in the secretaries' own homes, and will also give them private telephone lines. As the secretaries take care of their household chores, from time to time they will check the incoming dictation units to see if there is any typing to be done. If there is, they will sit at their terminal, copy the dictation, and note down its location in the computer file so that the boss can find it.

On the other end, the businessperson will look at the material that the secretaries put into the computer terminal, on a video display unit. Using a terminal keyboard, they can add any needed corrections themselves. If they have changed their mind about what they want to say, they can make more changes by phoning them into a remote dictation unit for a secretary to type later. Even when the papers are finally finished, they can stay in the computer to be passed along to other people in the company by video display units on their computer terminals. If for some reason paper copies are needed, they can easily be made on an automatic printer at the speed of 1500 words or more per minute.

The businessperson's company will have a magnetic tape microfiche system to store their records. All active records will be kept in computer storage banks that are easy to use. The advantage of this system is that the entire active file can be pulled from any terminal in the company — letters, reports, catalogs, and so forth — in seconds.

One new exciting invention is the speed compressor. You know how a phonograph record sounds if you increase the rate of speed; the voice on the record comes out sounding something like Donald Duck. When the speed compressor speeds

Today large businesses have computers and microfiche information banks; tomorrow even the smallest business will take advantage of these and many more advancements.

up the rate of recorded speech, it does not change the pitch. When the tape is played the voice on the tape is talking faster, but sounds the same as natural speech. A businessperson can listen to a tape recording of a conference in half the time it would have taken to attend the conference in person. The speech compressor also works on recorded phone messages. Reports and memos that are now written on paper could be recorded and listened to at twice the speed used in reading them. This recorded information can be played back at any time that it is convenient.

Television, calculators and photocopiers already exist. In future years they will find their way into the office, making the usual nine-to-five office day out of date.

Our businessperson will no longer need an office, or a room downtown, because they will carry their office with them. It fits inside a briefcase and includes a portable computer terminal that can be hooked up by any telephone to the company's central computer. They will also carry a microfiche viewer and a pocket-size dictation machine. This means they can conduct office business whether they are on an airplane, driving in a car, or sitting in their own kitchen. This unit has a special attachment that holds the dictation and transmits it at

high speed by telephone to the secretary at home.

Electronic message sending will also change messenger and mail delivery systems. There will always be a need for written reports in business, but they will be speeded on their way by computer-controlled mailing equipment that will print out the address, stuff the envelope, stamp it, seal it and sort it by cities before the postman ever comes to collect it.

Written messages will also be sent electronically from the company's computer to a computer at the other end. A businessperson in Los Angeles can send a message to the Paris office electronically on the company computer through a message routing satellite. The message will arrive minutes later, instead of the five or six days for mail delivery that it now takes.

Another help to the secretaries working in their homes will be computers with built-in dictionaries. These computers will automatically check spelling and have access to memory banks that will locate statistics and quotations so that the secretaries will no longer have to do this. If the businessperson wants to know the yield per acre of the wheat fields of Kansas, the secretary will only have to press the right button and in seconds have the information that is needed.

Tomorrow's businesspeople will also be able to get around much easier than today. Rather than waiting for commerical air flights to take them where they want to go, the automated features of tomorrow's aircraft will let them fly their own small planes.

The business plane of the future will be used more, and be more efficient, because of new engine developments.

It is believed that the major growth in professionally flown aircraft between now and the turn of the century will be in turbo prop and executive-use helicopters. Helicopters will increase the executive's ability to move around quickly, with the effect of adding to management's time.

But eventually even this form of chauffered transportation will give way to business people being able to transport themselves.

In the far future, the business people will be in the same position as every other type of worker; their business hours will shrink and play time will grow. The big question is, can we change our whole way of life by learning to use our free time wisely and enjoy our hours of work? If we are going to make the next giant step forward, we will have to do it.

GLOSSARY
OF TERMS USED IN
FUTURE BUSINESS

ARTIFACTS — A simple object made or changed by man, usually referring to a past civilization.

BIOCHEMICAL — Involves chemical reactions in living organisms.

BIOCONVERSION — Changing of living tissue.

BIONICS — Man-made physcial parts.

FILAMENT — A thin, thread like object.

MARICULTURE — Sea farming.

MICROBIOLOGY — Biology that deals with tiny (microscopic) forms of life.

MICROFICHE — A sheet of film containing small images of printed pages.

NUCLEAR FISSION — Energy produced by "breaking up" uranium or plutonium.

NUCLEAR FUSION — Energy produced by "joining" or "melting" hydrogen nuclei to make helium.

PLANETOID — Asteroid. The remains of an unformed planet. The planetoid belt lies between Jupiter and Mars.

SIMULATE — To give the appearance of, to imitate.

SPHERICAL — Shaped like a ball.

ABOUT THE AUTHOR

Harriette Sheffer Abels was born December 1, 1926 in Port Chester, New York. She attended Furman University, Greenville, South Carolina for one year. In addition to having her poetry published in the Furman literary magazine, she had her first major literary success while at the University. She wrote, produced and directed a three act musical comedy that was a smash hit!

At the age of twenty she moved to California, where she worked as a medical secretary for four years. In September, 1949, she married Robert Hamilton Abels, a manufacturers sales representative.

She began writing professionally in September, 1963. Her first major story was published in **Highlights For Children** in March, 1964, and her second appeared in **Jack and Jill** a short while later. She has been selling stories and articles ever since. Her first book was published by Ginn & Co., for the Magic Circle Program, in 1970.

Harriette and her husband love to travel and are looking forward to their annual trip to Europe. While travel doesn't leave much time for writing, Harriette does try to write at least something every day. When at home a sunporch serves as her office, but she confesses that most of her serious writing is done while stretched out on her bed.

The Abels have three children - Barbara Heidi, David Mark, and Carol Susan, and three dogs - Coco, Bon Bon, and Ginger Ale.

OUR FUTURE WORLD

DATE DUE

APR. 17			
APR. 24			